TALLINN

UNVEILED

The Ultimate Travel Guide for Your Wanderlust,
Whether Luxe or Thrifty

Eric J. Richardson

Copyright © Eric J.Richardson, 2023

All rights reserved. Except for brief quotations in critical reviews and certain other noncommercial uses permitted by copyright law, no part of this publication may be reproduced, distributed, or transmitted in any form or by any means, including photocopying, recording, or other electronic or mechanical methods, without the prior written permission of the publisher.

Table Of Contents

Introduction..4
    Getting to know Tallinn...8

Chapter 1: Getting Ready For Your Trip................... 13
    Deciding the Best Time For Your Trip..................... 13
    Know The Entry Requirements.............................. 16
    Best Fashion Advice and Things To Pack.............. 18
    Weather and How To Prepare for It........................ 21
    Things To Avoid in Tallinn.. 25
    Some practical Estonian idioms and terminologies used in Tallinn.. 28
    Customs and Cultural Etiquettes to Be Aware Of... 31

Chapter 2: Arriving In Tallinn.......................................35
    The Best Way To Get To Tallinn..............................35
    Tallinn on Arrival and How to Get to Your Lodge.... 38
    Settling Down: The Best Accommodations in Tallinn. 42
    Transportation Options in Tallinn............................. 49

Chapter 3: Famous Architectural Wonders and Tourist Attraction Sites in Tallinn.......................59

Chapter 4: Outdoor And Sporting Activities in Tallinn.. 76

Chapter 5: Best Restaurants and Bars in Tallinn.... 84

    Olde Hansa... 87

    Bottleneck... 89

    F-Hoone.. 91

    Noa.. 93

    Kompressor.. 95

    Peppersack... 97

    Manna... 100

    Bars... 104

Chapter 6: Best Souvenirs and Places To Buy Them in Tallinn... 114

    Vana Tallinn:... 114

    Juniper wood products:.. 114

    Knitwear:... 115

    Viking dolls:.. 115

    Kalevala Jewelry:... 115

    Handmade ceramics:.. 116

    Where to Buy Them.. 117

Conclusion and Added Essential Information....... 120

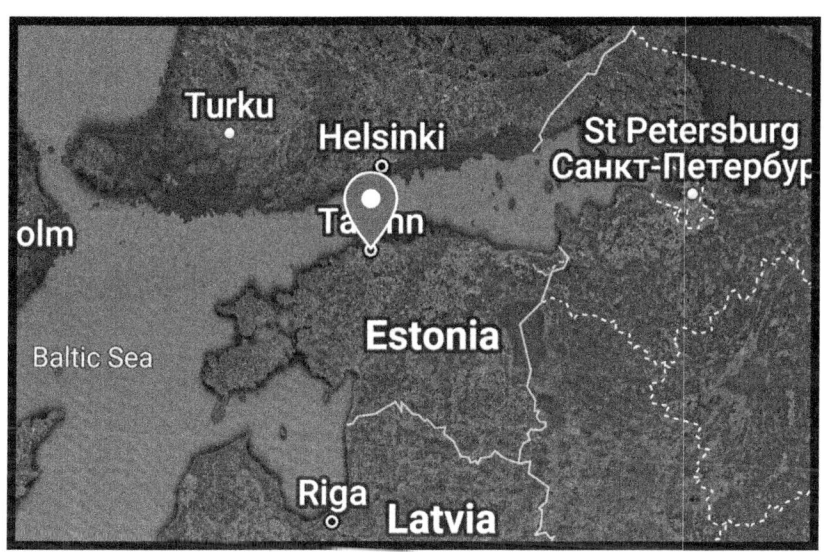

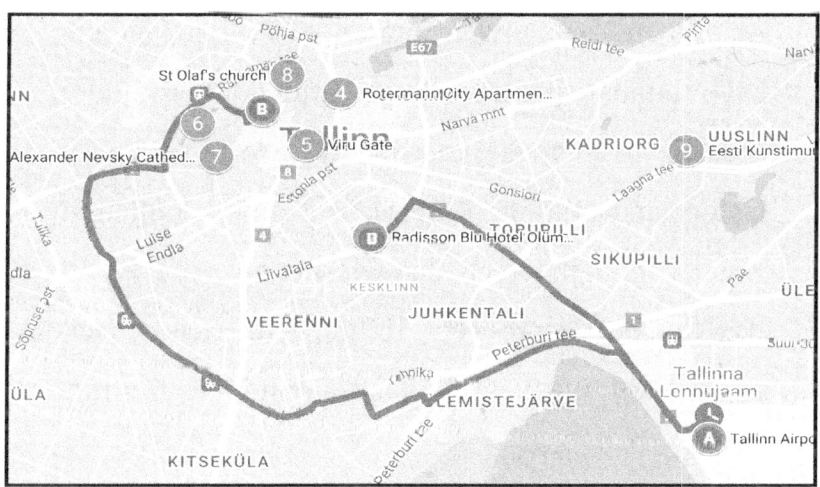

Introduction

Every city in the world has its characteristics, culture, and customs that make it unique and captivating. But some cities possess an undeniable charm, an enchantment that reaches deep into your soul and leaves an indelible mark on your heart. Tallinn, the capital of Estonia, is one such city.

As you embark on your journey to Tallinn, you may have certain expectations—a yearning for adventure, a desire to immerse yourself in a world steeped in history and folklore, or perhaps a simple longing to wander through streets that whisper tales of the past. And let me assure you, Tallinn will exceed every expectation, weaving its spell around you from the moment you arrive.

As you step onto the cobbled streets of Tallinn's Old Town, you'll be transported to a bygone era. The medieval architecture, with its towering spires and ancient stone walls, creates a sense of wonder and anticipation. You'll find yourself captivated by the narrow alleyways that wind through the city, each revealing hidden courtyards and secret gardens, waiting to be discovered.

But Tallinn is not just a city frozen in time. It is a living, breathing entity that seamlessly blends the old with the new. Venture beyond the medieval walls, and you'll find a vibrant and dynamic city, pulsating with energy. Modern art galleries, trendy cafes, and innovative design studios stand side by side with centuries-old churches and traditional taverns.

Throughout your stay in Tallinn, prepare to be embraced by a sense of warmth and hospitality that is intrinsic to the Estonian people. The locals will welcome you with open arms, eager to share their stories, traditions, and a taste of their world-renowned cuisine. Indulge in hearty meals of smoked fish, hearty soups, and delectable pastries, all lovingly prepared to tantalize your taste buds and nourish your soul.

As the days unfold, you'll find yourself falling deeper under Tallinn's spell. Lose yourself in the serenity of Kadriorg Park, where the whispering trees and blooming gardens provide a respite from the bustling city. Explore the rugged beauty of the nearby forests, where ancient tales of mythical creatures and mystical encounters come to life.

But it isn't simply nature that will take your breath away. Tallinn's cultural scene will captivate your senses, with its world-class museums, captivating theater performances, and live music festivals. Immerse yourself in the soul-stirring melodies of traditional Estonian folk music or lose yourself in the evocative sounds of contemporary artists pushing boundaries and reinventing the art form.

In Tallinn, your expectations will transform into something far greater—an emotional connection, an unbreakable bond with a city that will stay with you long after your journey ends. Whether you come seeking adventure, enlightenment, or simply a respite from the mundane, Tallinn will give you an experience that transcends time and space.

So, get ready to embark on a voyage of the heart and soul. Allow Tallinn to weave its magic around you, unraveling a tapestry of wonder and delight. Prepare to be moved, touched, and forever changed. Welcome to Tallinn, where dreams become reality and where the spirit of this ancient city will embrace you as one of its own.

Getting to know Tallinn

Tallinn is a city that weaves together history, culture, and natural beauty to create a tapestry unlike any other. Let me take you on a journey through time and space, as we delve into the captivating history, rich culture, diverse population, and unique geography of this beloved city.

History

Tallinn is a city with a long and rich history. It was first founded in the 12th century by the Danes, and it quickly became an important trading port. Tallinn was a member of the Hanseatic League, a powerful trading alliance, and it prospered during this time.

In the 16th century, Tallinn was conquered by the Swedes, and it remained under Swedish rule for over 200 years. In the 18th century, Tallinn was conquered by the Russians, and it remained under Russian rule until the end of World War I.

After World War I, Tallinn became the capital of the independent Republic of Estonia. In 1940, Estonia was annexed by the Soviet Union, and Tallinn became a part of the Soviet Union. Tallinn remained under Soviet rule until 1991 when Estonia regained its independence.

One of the most defining periods in Tallinn's history is its medieval era. The Old Town, a UNESCO World Heritage site, stands as a testament to this time. Its cobblestone streets wind through an architectural marvel, with Gothic spires, colorful merchant houses, and sturdy city walls that have witnessed centuries of triumphs and challenges.

Culture

Tallinn's culture is a captivating fusion of influences, blending ancient traditions with modern innovation. The Estonian people take great pride in preserving their heritage while embracing the opportunities of the present. Music plays a vital role in the cultural fabric of the city, with a deep appreciation for choral singing, traditional folk tunes, and contemporary sounds that reflect Estonia's resilient spirit.

The arts flourish in Tallinn, with numerous theaters, galleries, and cultural events throughout the year. From thought-provoking exhibitions to captivating theatrical performances, there is always something to inspire and captivate the soul. The city's creative energy extends beyond the traditional arts, encompassing design, literature, and culinary delights that showcase the creativity and vision of its people.

Population

Tallinn is home to a diverse population that adds vibrancy and depth to the city's tapestry. As the capital of Estonia, it attracts people from all walks of life, both native Estonians and expatriates from around the globe. Tallinn has a population of about 450,000 people. The majority of the population is

Estonian, but there are also large Russian, Ukrainian, and Finnish communities. Tallinn is a growing city, and the population is expected to continue to grow in the coming years.

Geography

Nestled on the southern coast of the Gulf of Finland, Tallinn boasts a picturesque setting that seamlessly merges natural beauty with urban sophistication. The city is surrounded by verdant forests, sparkling lakes, and a breathtaking coastline, offering an abundance of opportunities for outdoor exploration and recreation.

The landscape is defined by gentle slopes and rolling hills, providing panoramic views of the city and its surroundings. From the stunning coastal areas to the tranquil parks and nature reserves, Tallinn beckons nature enthusiasts to immerse themselves in its pristine beauty.

Tallinn's geography also includes the archipelago of nearby islands, such as Naissaar and Prangli, which offer idyllic retreats and a glimpse into traditional island life.

I can assure you that the history, culture, population, and geography of this remarkable city converge to create an experience like no other. From the echoes of medieval times in the cobblestone streets of the Old Town to the harmonious blend of cultures that define its people, Tallinn is a city that will seize your heart and leave an unforgettable imprint on your spirit.

Chapter 1:

Getting Ready For Your Trip

Deciding the Best Time For Your Trip

Deciding the best time for your trip to Tallinn is based on various factors. I would personally recommend visiting Tallinn during the spring or early autumn seasons. Here's why:

Spring (April to May): Spring in Tallinn brings a refreshing and vibrant atmosphere. The weather begins to warm up, and nature awakens with blooming flowers and budding trees. It's a delightful time to explore the city's parks and gardens, such as Kadriorg Park, as they come alive with colorful displays. The streets are less crowded compared to the peak summer season, allowing you to enjoy the city's attractions at a more leisurely pace. Additionally, you can catch Tallinn Music Week, a renowned music festival that celebrates both local and international talent, adding an extra touch of cultural immersion to your visit.

Early Autumn (September to October): Early autumn in Tallinn offers mild weather, making it comfortable for outdoor activities. The parks and forests start to showcase their autumn colors, providing picturesque scenery for hikes and walks. Lahemaa National Park, with its ancient forests and rugged coastal cliffs, is particularly stunning during this season. The city's cultural scene comes alive with various events, such as Tallinn Restaurant Week, where you can indulge in culinary delights at discounted prices. It's also an ideal time to explore vibrant neighborhoods, like Kalamaja, and discover the local art and design scene.

Both spring and early autumn allow you to experience Tallinn with fewer crowds compared to the peak summer season. You'll have the opportunity to interact more closely with locals, enjoy shorter queues at popular attractions, and savor the city's authentic ambiance. Additionally, the shoulder seasons often offer more favorable prices for flights and accommodations, allowing you to make the most of your budget.

Of course, your personal preferences and interests should also be considered when planning your trip. If you enjoy winter activities, the snowy months can be magical, especially around the holiday season. Summer is vibrant and lively, with longer daylight hours and a wide range of festivals and outdoor events.

Ultimately, the choice of when to visit Tallinn depends on the experiences you seek and the atmosphere you prefer. Regardless of the season, Tallinn's charm and allure will captivate you, offering a unique blend of history, culture, and natural beauty that is sure to leave a lasting impression.

Know The Entry Requirements

Currently, the following are the entry requirements for tourists traveling to Tallinn, Estonia:

- Valid passport: Your passport must be valid for at least 6 months beyond your planned date of exit from Estonia.
- Visa: If you are a citizen of a country that requires a visa to enter Estonia, you will need to apply for a visa before you travel.
- Proof of vaccination: You must be fully vaccinated against COVID-19 to enter Estonia. You can show proof of vaccination

with your vaccination certificate or a negative COVID-19 test result.
- Travel insurance: You are required to have travel insurance that covers medical expenses in case you get sick or injured while in Estonia.

Please note that these requirements are subject to change, so it is always best to check with the Estonian embassy or consulate in your country before you travel.

Here are some additional tips for entry into Tallinn:
- Make sure you have all of your travel documents ready before you go to the airport.
- Be prepared to show your vaccination certificate or negative COVID-19 test result at the border.
- Have your travel insurance information handy in case you need to use it.

- Be patient and polite when dealing with border control officials.

Best Fashion Advice and Things To Pack

I'm excited to share some fashion advice to help you make the most of your trip to Tallinn. Make sure to keep the following in mind while planning your wardrobe:

Layering is Key: Tallinn's weather can be quite unpredictable, especially in spring and autumn. It's best to dress in layers, so you can easily adjust to changing temperatures throughout the day. Start with a base layer, such as a comfortable t-shirt or blouse, and add a light sweater or cardigan. Top it off with a waterproof or windproof jacket, especially if you plan to explore the city on foot.

Comfortable Shoes: Tallinn's old town is full of charming cobblestone streets, which can be uneven to walk on. Opt for comfortable shoes with good support, as you'll likely be doing a lot of walking while exploring the city's attractions and neighborhoods. Choose shoes that are both stylish and practical to keep your feet happy throughout the day.

Casual and Versatile Attire: Tallinn has a relaxed and casual atmosphere, so you can feel comfortable wearing a variety of outfits. Pack a mix of versatile clothing items that can be easily mixed and matched. Jeans, skirts, shorts, or dresses paired with t-shirts, blouses, or shirts are all great options. This will allow you to adapt your outfit to different activities and occasions.

Embrace Local Fashion: Estonians have a unique sense of style, often blending contemporary fashion with traditional elements. Consider incorporating some local fashion pieces into your wardrobe to embrace the Estonian aesthetic. Look for locally designed clothing or accessories, such as hand-knitted sweaters, woven scarves, or Baltic amber jewelry, which can add a touch of authenticity to your outfits.

Be Prepared for Rain: Tallinn is known for its occasional showers, so it's wise to pack a small, foldable umbrella or a lightweight raincoat. This will ensure that you're prepared for unexpected rain showers and can continue exploring the city without being caught off guard.

Respectful Attire for Religious Sites: If you plan to visit churches or other religious sites in Tallinn, it's advisable to dress modestly out of respect for religious customs. Avoid wearing revealing clothing or shorts and consider carrying a scarf or shawl to cover your shoulders if necessary.

Accessories and Essentials: Don't forget to pack essential accessories like sunglasses, a hat or cap to protect yourself from the sun, and a comfortable backpack or crossbody bag to carry your belongings while exploring the city.

Remember, the most important aspect of your fashion choices is to feel comfortable and confident in what you wear. Dressing appropriately for the weather and activities will ensure that you can fully enjoy your time in Tallinn without any fashion-related concerns.

Weather and How To Prepare for It

Tallinn experiences a temperate climate with distinct seasons. Here's a breakdown of the weather and the preparations you can make:

Spring (April to May): Spring in Tallinn brings a mix of mild and chilly weather. Average temperatures range from 5°C to 15°C (41°F to 59°F). While the days gradually become warmer, it's still advisable to layer your clothing. Prepare for occasional rain showers by packing a waterproof jacket and an umbrella. It's also a good idea to have a light sweater or cardigan to add warmth when needed. Comfortable walking shoes are a must, as said earlier, you'll likely be exploring the city's attractions on foot.

Summer (June to August): Summer is the most pleasant and popular season in Tallinn. Average temperatures range from 15°C to 25°C (59°F to 77°F), but occasionally, it can reach higher temperatures. The days are long, providing ample daylight for exploring. Light and breathable clothing, such as t-shirts, shorts, skirts, and summer dresses, are ideal for the warm weather. Don't forget your sunglasses, sunscreen, and a hat to protect yourself from the sun's rays. However, it's wise to carry a light sweater or jacket for cooler evenings or sudden temperature drops.

Autumn (September to October): Autumn in Tallinn is characterized by cooler temperatures and changing foliage. Average temperatures range from 5°C to 15°C (41°F to 59°F) during this season. Layering is crucial during autumn as the weather can vary throughout the day. Have a mix of long-sleeved shirts, light sweaters, and jackets to adapt to the changing temperatures. It's also advisable to have a waterproof outer layer, as autumn brings more frequent rainfall. Comfortable shoes and an umbrella are essential for strolling through the city.

Winter (November to March): Winter in Tallinn can be quite cold, with temperatures ranging from

-5°C to 0°C (23°F to 32°F) on average. Snowfall is common, resulting in a winter wonderland. It's important to dress warmly in thermal layers, sweaters, heavy coats, scarves, hats, gloves, and warm socks. Waterproof and insulated footwear is essential to keep your feet dry and warm. Don't forget to protect your face and eyes from the cold wind with a scarf and sunglasses. Additionally, consider packing hand and foot warmers for extra comfort during extended periods outdoors.

Regardless of the season, it's advisable to check the weather forecast a few days before your trip to Tallinn. This will help you make any necessary adjustments to your packing and ensure that you're well-prepared for the specific weather conditions during your visit.

In summary, layering your clothing, packing a mix of versatile garments, having waterproof outerwear, and wearing comfortable footwear are key elements for preparing for the weather in Tallinn.

Things To Avoid in Tallinn

Here are some things I advise you to avoid in Tallinn:

- **Pickpockets:** Tallinn is a relatively safe city, but there are still pickpockets around, especially in crowded areas like the Old Town. Be sure to keep your valuables close to you and don't flash your money around.
- **Overpriced restaurants:** The Old Town is full of overpriced restaurants that cater to tourists. If you're looking for a good meal at a reasonable price, you'll need to venture outside of the Old Town.
- **Rip-off taxis:** There have been reports of taxis overcharging tourists. If you're taking a

taxi, be sure to agree on the price before you get in the car.

- **Nightclubs that cater to tourists:** Tallinn has a vibrant nightlife scene, but several nightclubs cater to tourists. These clubs can be expensive and the crowds can be rowdy. If you're looking for a more authentic Tallinn experience, you'll want to avoid these clubs.
- **The black market:** Tallinn has a small black market, but it's best to avoid it. The goods on the black market are often stolen or counterfeit, and you could get scammed.
- Walking alone at night: Tallinn is a safe city, but it's always best to be cautious, especially at night. If you're walking alone at night, be sure to stay in well-lit areas and avoid alleyways.
- Drink spiking: There have been reports of drink spiking in Tallinn, especially in bars and clubs. If you're going to drink, be sure to

keep an eye on your drink and don't leave it unattended.

- Getting into fights: Tallinn is a friendly city, but there have been reports of tourists getting into fights, especially in bars and clubs. If you're drinking, be sure to drink responsibly and avoid getting into arguments.
- Street Solicitations and Scams: Be cautious of street solicitors who may try to sell you counterfeit products or engage in other scams. Avoid engaging with strangers who approach you with suspicious offers or requests for money. Use common sense and trust your instincts when dealing with unfamiliar individuals.
- Unofficial Currency Exchange: When exchanging currency, it's advisable to use official currency exchange offices or banks. Avoid exchanging money with individuals on the street or in unofficial establishments, as

they may offer poor exchange rates or engage in fraudulent practices. It's always a good idea to compare rates and fees before making any currency exchanges.

Some practical Estonian idioms and terminologies used in Tallinn

Here are some practical Estonian idioms and terminologies used in Tallinn that you should be aware of:

1. Tere - This simple word means "Hello" in Estonian. It's a common greeting and a polite way to start conversations with locals.

2. Aitäh - "Aitäh" is the Estonian word for "Thank you." It's always appreciated to express gratitude when receiving assistance or service.

3. **Palun** - "Palun" translates to "Please" in English. It's a polite way to make requests or ask for something.
4. Kuidas läheb? - This phrase means "How are you?" It's a friendly way to inquire about someone's well-being and can be used as a greeting.
5. Nägemist - When parting ways, you can say "Nägemist," which means "Goodbye" in Estonian. It's a nice way to say goodbye.
6. **Terviseks** - This phrase means "Cheers!" or "To your health!" It's commonly used when raising a toast during social gatherings.
7. Eesti keel - "Eesti keel" means "Estonian language." While many locals in Tallinn speak English, making an effort to learn a few Estonian phrases can be appreciated by locals and add a personal touch to your interactions.

8. Suur aitäh - "Suur aitäh" translates to "Thank you very much." It's an expression of deep gratitude and appreciation.
9. Kallis - "Kallis" means "dear" or "darling" and is used as a term of endearment. You may hear people addressing their loved ones or close friends using this term.
10. Ootan sind - "Ootan sind" translates to "I'm waiting for you." It's a phrase you can use to express anticipation for someone's arrival or meeting.

Remember, while it's not essential to become fluent in Estonian, knowing a few basic phrases can go a long way in connecting with locals, showing respect for the local culture, and making your time in Tallinn more enjoyable. Estonians are generally appreciative of visitors who make an effort to engage with their language and traditions.

Customs and Cultural Etiquettes to Be Aware Of

When it comes to customs and cultural etiquette that will help you navigate the city and interact with locals respectfully, the key is to be observant, open-minded, and willing to embrace the customs and traditions of the Estonian people.

1. Greetings: When meeting someone, it's customary to greet them with a handshake and make direct eye contact. In more informal settings, a nod or a simple "Tere" (Hello) is also acceptable.

2. Punctuality: Estonians value punctuality, so it's important to be on time for scheduled appointments, meetings, or tours. If you anticipate being late, it's polite to inform the person in advance.

3. Personal Space: Estonians appreciate their personal space and tend to maintain a

relatively larger physical distance during conversations compared to some other cultures. Respect this space and avoid unnecessary physical contact unless you have a close relationship with the person.

4. Shoes Off Indoors: It's customary to remove your shoes when entering someone's home or certain establishments, such as saunas. Look for a shoe rack or observe if others have taken off their shoes before entering a place.

5. Dining Etiquette: When invited to someone's home for a meal, it's customary to remove your shoes upon entering. Wait to be seated and allow the host to initiate the meal. It's polite to try a bit of everything served and to compliment the host's cooking. Finish your plate as leaving food behind may be considered wasteful.

6. Public Behavior: Estonians tend to be reserved and private in public spaces. Avoid

speaking loudly or making excessive noise, especially in quiet areas like libraries or public transportation. Respect the environment and keep it clean by using designated bins for waste disposal.

7. Respect for Nature: Estonia has a strong connection with nature, and Tallinn is no exception. When visiting parks, gardens, or natural areas, it's essential to respect the environment and adhere to any rules or guidelines provided. Avoid trash and leave the place in the same condition that you found it.

8. Sauna Etiquette: Saunas holds a special place in Estonian culture. If you have the opportunity to experience a sauna, it's customary to go naked or wear a towel. Remember to sit on a towel to maintain hygiene and avoid sitting directly on the wooden benches. It's polite to follow the lead

of the locals regarding sauna rituals and practices.

By following these customs and cultural etiquettes, you'll be able to engage with the local community in Tallinn and have a more immersive and respectful experience during your visit.

Chapter 2:

Arriving In Tallinn

The Best Way To Get To Tallinn

Tallinn is a popular tourist destination and it is well-connected and offers various transportation options for travelers from different parts of the world. The best way for you to get to Tallinn depends on your preferences, budget, and starting location. Let's explore the best way for you to get to Tallinn.

By Air: The most convenient and time-efficient way to reach Tallinn is by air. The Lennart Meri Tallinn Airport (TLL) serves as the main gateway to the city and is located just a short distance from the city center. The airport offers a wide range of international flights, connecting Tallinn to major cities in Europe and beyond. Airlines such as Finnair, Lufthansa, Turkish Airlines, and Ryanair operate regular flights to Tallinn, making it easily accessible from various destinations. With its modern facilities, efficient services, and direct flight options, flying to Tallinn is a popular choice for travelers looking for convenience and comfort.

By Ferry: If you prefer a more scenic and leisurely journey, traveling to Tallinn by ferry is an excellent choice. Tallinn is located on the shores of the Baltic Sea, and the city's passenger terminals are well-connected to neighboring countries such as Finland and Sweden. Several ferry companies, including Tallink, Viking Line, and Eckerö Line, operate regular routes to Tallinn, offering a comfortable and enjoyable sea voyage. The ferries are equipped with amenities like restaurants, shops, and entertainment options, ensuring a pleasant journey.

The ferry connections from Helsinki, for example, are particularly popular and convenient. The journey takes approximately 2-3 hours, allowing you to relax and take in the beautiful views of the Baltic Sea. Once you arrive at the port in Tallinn, the city center is easily accessible by public transportation or a short taxi ride.

By Bus: For budget-conscious travelers or those who enjoy the flexibility of road travel, reaching Tallinn by bus is a viable option. Several bus companies, including Lux Express, Eurolines, and Ecolines, operate regular routes to Tallinn from various European cities. The buses are comfortable, equipped with modern amenities such as Wi-Fi and onboard restrooms, and offer affordable fares. The bus terminals in Tallinn are conveniently located near the city center, making it easy to access your accommodation and explore the city's attractions upon arrival.

By Train: Although train travel is not the most popular way to reach Tallinn, it can still be an option depending on your starting point. The Baltic Railway connects Tallinn to cities like Moscow, St. Petersburg, and Riga, offering scenic journeys through the Estonian countryside. While train connections may not be as extensive as air or ferry options, they can provide a unique and leisurely travel experience for those who enjoy train travel.

Whichever mode of transportation you choose, rest assured that Tallinn awaits you with its captivating beauty and rich cultural heritage.

Tallinn on Arrival and How to Get to Your Lodge

Upon landing at Tallinn Airport, you will proceed through immigration and passport control. Make sure to have your valid passport and any necessary visas ready for inspection. Citizens of certain countries may require a visa to enter Estonia, so it's essential to check the visa requirements before your trip.

After passing through immigration, you will head to the baggage claim area to get your belongings. Tallinn Airport has well-organized baggage claim belts, and the process is usually efficient. Once you have retrieved your bags, you can move on to the customs control area. Customs checks in Tallinn are generally straightforward, with random screenings conducted to ensure compliance with customs regulations.

Getting to Your Lodge: Tallinn Airport is located approximately 4 kilometers from the city center, and you have several options to reach your lodge:

1. Taxi: Outside the airport building, taxis are easily accessible. Official taxis are metered, and the rates are displayed on the window or

dashboard. The taxi fare to the city center is around €15. The journey from the airport to the city center takes around 10-15 minutes, depending on traffic conditions.

2. Ride-Hailing Services: Popular ride-hailing services such as Bolt and Uber operate in Tallinn. You can download the respective apps on your mobile phone and request a ride from the airport. The apps provide estimated fares and waiting times, making it convenient to arrange transportation to your lodge.

3. Public Transportation: Tallinn Airport is well-connected to the city's public transportation network. Bus number 2 operates between the airport and the city center, making stops at various key locations. The bus stop is located just outside the terminal, and you can purchase tickets from the driver or use a contactless payment

method. The bus fare is around €2. The journey to the city center takes approximately 20-30 minutes, depending on traffic.

4. Airport Shuttle Services: Some hotels in Tallinn provide airport shuttle services for their guests. If you have arranged accommodation with a hotel offering this service, check with them in advance for shuttle availability and reservation procedures.

It's advisable to have the address of your lodge written down or saved on your mobile device, as it will make it easier for the taxi driver or ride-hailing service to navigate to your destination. Most accommodations in Tallinn are familiar to local drivers, but having the exact address ensures a smooth and hassle-free transfer.

Settling Down: The Best Accommodations in Tallinn

Tallinn offers a wide range of options to suit different budgets, preferences, and travel styles. Whether you're looking for luxury, comfort, or a more budget-friendly stay, there's something for everyone. Here are the main types of accommodations you can consider in Tallinn:

Hotels: Tallinn boasts a variety of hotels ranging from luxurious five-star establishments to cozy boutique hotels and budget-friendly options. The city center, especially the Old Town, is home to numerous hotels, offering convenient access to major attractions, restaurants, and shopping areas. Hotels in Tallinn often provide amenities such as on-site restaurants, bars, fitness centers, and spa facilities.

Guesthouses: Guesthouses are popular among budget-conscious travelers and those looking for a more homely atmosphere. These accommodations are typically smaller in scale and offer comfortable rooms with shared facilities. Guesthouses are scattered throughout the city, including the Old Town, city outskirts, and residential areas, providing an opportunity to experience local neighborhoods and interact with friendly hosts.

Apartments and Vacation Rentals: Renting an apartment or vacation rental is an excellent option for travelers seeking a more independent and immersive experience. There are various platforms and agencies offering apartments in Tallinn, allowing you to choose from a range of sizes, locations, and amenities. Renting an apartment gives you the flexibility to cook your meals, have more space, and live like a local during your stay.

Hostels: Tallinn has several well-maintained hostels that cater to budget travelers, backpackers, and solo adventurers. Hostels offer dormitory-style accommodation with shared facilities such as kitchens, common areas, and laundry facilities. They are a great way to meet fellow travelers and often organize social events or city tours. The majority of hostels are located in or near the city center, making it convenient to explore Tallinn's attractions.

Bed and Breakfasts: Bed and breakfast establishments provide a comfortable and cozy environment, often in family-run homes or small guesthouses. These accommodations typically offer breakfast as part of the stay and may have limited rooms, ensuring personalized attention and a warm atmosphere. Bed and breakfasts can be found both in the city center and in the surrounding suburban areas.

Spa Hotels: If you're seeking relaxation and pampering, Tallinn has several spa hotels to choose from. These accommodations offer a combination of comfortable rooms and wellness facilities, such as saunas, hot tubs, and massage services. Spa hotels are perfect for those looking to unwind and rejuvenate during their stay in Tallinn.

It's worth noting that regardless of the type of accommodation you choose, it's advisable to book in advance, especially during peak tourist seasons or major events. This ensures you have a wider selection of options and secures your preferred choice.

Some of the best accommodations in Tallinn

Budget:

- **Old Town Hostel:** This hostel is located in the heart of the Old Town, and it's a great option for budget travelers. It has a shared

kitchen, a common room, and laundry facilities. Dorm beds cost €15 per night.
- **SleepWell Hostel:** This hostel is located in the city center, and it's another great option for budget travelers. It has a shared kitchen, a common room, and laundry facilities. Dorm beds start at €10 per night.
- **AHHAA Hostel:** This hostel is located in the Telliskivi Creative City district, and it's a great option for travelers who want to experience Tallinn's creative scene. It has a shared kitchen, a common room, and laundry facilities. Dorm beds start at €12 per night.

Mid-range:
- **Kalamaja Guesthouse:** This guesthouse is located in the Kalamaja district, and it's a great option for travelers who want to experience Tallinn's hipster side. It has a kitchen, a living room, and a washing machine. Apartments start at €70 per night.

- **Old Town Inn:** This guesthouse is located in the Old Town, and it's a great option for travelers who want to be in the heart of the action. It has a kitchen, a living room, and a washing machine. Apartments start at €100 per night.
- **Rotermann City Apartment:** This apartment is located in the Rotermann Quarter, and it's a great option for travelers who want to be in a trendy neighborhood. It has a kitchen, a living room, and a washing machine. Apartments start at €120 per night.

Luxury:

- **Radisson Blu Hotel Olümpia:** This 5-star hotel is located in the heart of the city center, just a short walk from the Old Town. It has a rooftop pool with amazing views of the city, a spa, and a fitness center. Rooms start at €150 per night.

- **Sokos Hotel Viru:** This 4-star hotel is also located in the city center, and it's one of the most iconic hotels in Tallinn. It has a casino, a bar, and a restaurant. Rooms start at €100 per night.
- **Hotel Telegraaf:** This 4-star hotel is located in the Old Town, and it's housed in a beautifully restored Art Nouveau building. It has a spa, a fitness center, and a rooftop terrace with views of the Old Town. Rooms start at €120 per night.

Hidden gems:

- **Meriton Old Town Garden Hotel:** This hotel is located in the Old Town, and it's a great option for travelers who want to stay in a historic building. It has a spa, a fitness center, and a rooftop terrace with views of the Old Town. Rooms start at €150 per night.
- **Bob W. Tallinn Telliskivi:** This hotel is located in the Telliskivi Creative City district,

and it's a great option for travelers who want to experience Tallinn's creative scene. It has a bar, a restaurant, and a rooftop terrace with views of the city. Rooms start at €120 per night.

- **Revelton Suites Tallinn:** This apartment hotel is located in the city center, and it's a great option for travelers who want more space and privacy. It has a kitchen, a living room, and a washing machine. Apartments start at €150 per night.

Transportation Options in Tallinn

Public transportation

Tallinn has a well-developed public transportation system, which includes:

Buses

Buses are a great way to get around Tallinn, especially if you're visiting the suburbs.

The buses in Tallinn are yellow, and they run from 5:30 am to 11:30 pm. They're wheelchair accessible and there are designated bus lanes throughout the city, so they tend to run on time.

You can buy tickets for buses at ticket machines at bus stops, tram stops, and the metro station. A single ticket costs €2.00, and a day ticket costs €5.50.

The main bus stations in Tallinn are Hobujaama, Viru, and Kaubamaja. These stations are all located in the city center, so they're a great place to start your exploration of Tallinn.

The buses in Tallinn are operated by Tallinna Linnatranspordi AS (TLT), the same company that operates the trams and trolleybuses in Tallinn.

Trams

Trams are a great way to get around Tallinn, especially if you're visiting the city center or the Old Town. They're also a very affordable way to travel.

The trams are green and white, and they run from 5:30 am to 11:30 pm. They're wheelchair accessible, and there are designated tram lanes throughout the city.

You can buy tickets for trams at ticket machines at tram stops, bus stops, and the metro station. A single ticket costs €2.00, and a day ticket costs €6.00.

The main tram stations in Tallinn are Hobujaama, Viru, and Kadriorg. These stations are all located in the city center.

Trolleybuses

Trolleybuses are also a great way to get around Tallinn, especially if you're visiting the Mustamäe district. They're also very affordable.

The trolleybuses are blue and white, and they run from 5:30 am to 11:30 pm. They're wheelchair accessible, and there are designated trolley bus lanes throughout the city, so they tend to run on time.

You can buy tickets for trolleybuses at ticket machines at trolley bus stops, bus stops, and the metro station. A single ticket costs €2.00, and a day ticket costs €6.00.

The main trolley bus stations in Tallinn are Hobujaama, Viru, and Mustamäe. These stations are all located in the city center, so you can also start your exploration of Tallinn with them.

The trolleybuses in Tallinn are powered by electricity, which is collected from overhead wires. This makes them a very environmentally friendly way to travel.

Here are some additional tips for using the trolleybuses in Tallinn:
- If you're planning on using the trolleybuses a lot, you may want to consider getting a day ticket. In time, this will save you money.

- The trolleybuses can get crowded during rush hour, so it's a good idea to give yourself plenty of time to get to your destination.
- If you're traveling with a stroller or wheelchair, be sure to board the trolley bus at the front door. There is more space for strollers and wheelchairs at the front of the trolley bus.

Taxi

If you're in a hurry or if you're traveling with a lot of luggage, Taxis are a great way to get around Tallinn. They're also a bit more expensive than public transportation, but they're still relatively affordable.

You can hail a taxi from the street, or you can book one in advance through the app.

The fares for taxis in Tallinn are based on a meter, and they start at €2.50. The fare per kilometer is €0.40, and there is a waiting fee of €0.20 per minute.

The taxis in Tallinn are generally very good, and the drivers are friendly and helpful. However, it's always a good idea to check the meter before you get in the taxi, just to make sure that you're not being overcharged.

Walking and Biking

Walking is another great way to get around Tallinn, and it's also a great way to see the city. The city center is relatively compact, so it's easy to walk from one point to another. And there are plenty of pedestrian-friendly streets and paths to explore.

Tallinn is a great city for biking. There are a lot of dedicated bike paths, and the city is relatively flat, so it's easy to get around.

Renting A Car

Renting a car in Tallinn can be a great option if you prefer to have the freedom to explore the city and its surrounding areas at your own pace.

The city has a good road network, and it's easy to get around.

There are several car rental companies in Tallinn, so you'll be able to find one that fits your needs and budget. The most popular car rental companies in Tallinn are Europcar, Sixt, and Hertz.

When you rent a car in Tallinn, you'll need to provide your driver's license, passport, and credit card. You'll also need to pay a deposit, which is usually the same as the daily rental rate.

The cost of renting a car in Tallinn varies depending on the type of car you rent, the length of your rental, and the time of year. You can expect to pay anywhere from €20 to €100 per day for a rental car in Tallinn. The minimum age to rent a car in Tallinn is usually 21 or 25, depending on the rental company. However, some companies may have age restrictions or additional fees for drivers under 25. You will need to purchase a collision damage waiver

(CDW) if you want to be covered for any damage to the rental car.

If you're planning on renting a car in Tallinn, it's a good idea to book your rental in advance, especially during the peak season. You can book your rental car online or by calling the car rental company.

Driving in Tallinn

Driving in Tallinn is relatively easy, but there are a few things you should keep in mind.

- The speed limit in the city center is 50 km/h (31 mph), and the speed limit outside of the city center is 90 km/h (56 mph).
- Be aware of pedestrians and cyclists, as they have the right of way in many cases.
- Parking might be challenging, particularly in the city center. There are several parking garages and pay-and-display lots, but they can be expensive.

- The traffic can be heavy during rush hour, so it's a good idea to plan your route accordingly.
- Be aware of the traffic laws in Tallinn. Among the most significant rules are:
  - Do not drink and drive. The legal limit for blood alcohol content (BAC) in Estonia is 0.02%.
  - Use your turn signals.
  - Do not use your phone while driving.
  - Obey the speed limit.
  - Be aware of pedestrians and cyclists.

Rush hours in Tallinn are typically from 7 am to 9 am and from 4 pm to 6 pm, Monday through Friday. The heaviest traffic is usually found on the main roads leading into and out of the city center. Some specific times when traffic is especially heavy are:

- 7:30 am to 8:30 am: This is the busiest time of the morning, as people are commuting to work or school.

- 4:30 pm to 5:30 pm: This is the busiest time of the evening, as people are commuting home from work or school.
- Friday afternoons: Traffic is often heavier on Friday afternoons, as people are leaving town for the weekend.

If you are planning on driving in Tallinn during rush hour, it is a good idea to plan your route accordingly.

Chapter 3:

Famous Architectural Wonders and Tourist Attraction Sites in Tallinn

The Tallinn Town Wall

The Tallinn Town Wall is one of the most iconic landmarks in Tallinn, and it is a UNESCO World Heritage Site. It is a massive defensive structure that was built in the 13th century to protect the city from attack. The wall is made of limestone, and it is about 1.85 kilometers long. It has 26 towers and two gates.

The Tallinn Town Wall is a popular tourist destination, and it is a great place to get a panoramic view of the city. You can walk along the wall, or you can climb up one of the towers. There are also several museums located in the towers, including the Kiek in de Kök, which is a military museum.

The Tallinn Town Wall is a reminder of our city's rich history, and it is a symbol of Tallinn's resilience. It has survived wars, fires, and earthquakes, and it continues to stand today as a testament to the strength of our city.

Here are some of the things you can do at the Tallinn Town Wall:

- Enjoy the sights of the city as you walk along the wall.
- Climb up one of the towers for a bird's eye view of Tallinn.
- Visit the Kiek in de Kök military museum.
- Learn about the history of the wall at one of the many information boards.
- Take a photo with the Tallinn Town Wall as the backdrop.
- Visit the Patkuli Viewing Platform, which offers stunning views of the wall and the city.

The Tallinn Town Wall is a great place to visit for a day out, and it is a must-see for any visitor to Tallinn.

How to visit the Tallinn Town Wall:

The Tallinn Town Wall is located in the Old Town, and it is easily accessible by foot. You can also take the bus or tram to Viru Street, which is just outside the wall. The wall is open to the public from 9:00 AM to 5:00 PM, and there is no admission fee.

Here are a few particular locations you can visit:

- Kiek in de Kök: This is a military museum that is located in one of the towers of the Tallinn Town Wall. It offers a great view of the city, and it has exhibits on the history of the wall and the city's defenses.

- Pikk Hermann: This is the tallest tower on the Tallinn Town Wall, and it offers panoramic views of the city. It is also the symbol of

Tallinn, and it is often used in the city's branding.
- Hellemann Tower: This is another tall tower of the Tallinn Town Wall, and it offers views of the city and the harbor. It is also a popular photography location.
- Nunnatorn: This is a small tower that is located near the Kiek in de Kök museum. It offers views of the city and the Patkuli Viewing Platform.

The Viru Gate

The Viru Gate is one of the most iconic landmarks in Tallinn, and it is a popular tourist destination. It is located in the eastern section of the Tallinn Town Wall, and it is one of the two remaining gates that were originally part of the city's defensive system. The gate was built in the 14th century, and it consists of two square towers that are connected by a curtain wall. The towers are about 30 meters tall, and they are topped with crenelated battlements.

The Viru Gate was originally used to control traffic into and out of the Old Town, and it also served as a defensive position in case of attack. The gate was heavily fortified, and it was equipped with cannons and other weapons.

Today, the Viru Gate is no longer used for defensive purposes, but it is still an important symbol of Tallinn. The gate is a popular tourist destination, and it is often used as a backdrop for photographs. The Viru Gate is also home to several shops and restaurants, and it is a popular place to visit for shopping and dining.

Here are some of the things you can do at the Viru Gate:
- Walk through the gate and imagine what it would have been like to pass through it in the 14th century.

- Visit the Viru Gate Museum, which tells the history of the gate and the Tallinn Town Wall.
- Take a photo with the Viru Gate as the backdrop.
- Do some shopping or dining in the shops and restaurants that are located in the Viru Gate.
- Visit the Viru Keskus shopping mall, which is located just outside the gate.

The Viru Gate is a great place to visit for a day out, and it is a must-see for any visitor to Tallinn.

How to visit the Viru Gate:

The Viru Gate is located in the eastern section of the Old Town, and it is easily accessible by foot. You can also take the bus or tram to Viru Street, which is just outside the gate. The gate is open to the public from 9:00 AM to 5:00 PM, and there is no admission fee.

Toompea Hill

Toompea Hill is the highest point in Tallinn, and it is home to many of the city's most important historical and cultural landmarks. The hill is crowned by the Toompea Castle, which has been the seat of the Estonian government since 1920. Other notable buildings on Toompea Hill include the Alexander Nevsky Cathedral, the House of the Parliament, and the Kiek in de Kök Museum.

Toompea Hill has been inhabited since the 9th century, and it has been the site of many important events in Estonian history. In the 13th century, the Danes built a castle on the hill, and it became the center of Danish rule in Estonia. In the 16th century, the castle was captured by the Russians, and it remained in Russian hands until 1918.

Today, Toompea Hill is a popular tourist destination, and it is a great place to learn about Estonian history and culture. You can visit the Toompea Castle, the

Alexander Nevsky Cathedral, and the Kiek in de Kök museum. You can also walk around the hill and enjoy the stunning views of Tallinn.

St. Olav's Church

St. Olav's Church is the tallest building in Tallinn, and it offers stunning views of the city from its 318-foot-high tower. The church was built in the 13th century, and it has been rebuilt several times since then. St. Olav's Church is a popular tourist destination, and it is also a significant religious landmark for Estonians.

The church is dedicated to Saint Olav, a Norwegian king who was martyred in 1030. The church was originally built in the Romanesque style, but it was later rebuilt in the Gothic style. The church's tower was added in the 16th century, and it is the tallest structure in Tallinn.

Kadriorg Park

Kadriorg Park is a beautiful park located in the northeastern part of Tallinn. The park was founded in the 1720s by Peter the Great, and it is home to several palaces, gardens, and fountains. Kadriorg Park is a popular spot for locals and tourists alike, and it is a great place to relax and enjoy the outdoors.

The park was originally designed by a French architect, and it is inspired by the Gardens of Versailles. The park is home to several palaces, including the Kadriorg Palace, which was built for Peter the Great's wife, Catherine I. The park also has several gardens, fountains, and sculptures.

Alexander Nevsky Cathedral

Alexander Nevsky Cathedral is an imposing Russian Orthodox cathedral that was built in the 19th century. The cathedral is dedicated to Saint Alexander Nevsky, a Russian military leader and saint. Alexander Nevsky Cathedral is a popular tourist destination, and it is also an important religious landmark for Russian speakers in Estonia.

The cathedral was built in the Russian Revival style, and it is one of the largest churches in Tallinn. The cathedral has a tall bell tower, and it is topped with a golden dome. The interior of the cathedral is decorated with beautiful mosaics and icons.

House of the Brotherhood of Blackheads

House of the Brotherhood of Blackheads is a historic building located in the Old Town of Tallinn. The building was built in the 14th century, and it was originally the headquarters of the Brotherhood of Blackheads, a guild of unmarried merchants and artisans. The House of the Brotherhood of Blackheads is now a museum, and it is a popular tourist destination.

The building is a beautiful example of Gothic architecture, and it is decorated with intricate carvings. The interior of the building is also beautifully decorated, and it houses several historical artifacts.

Kumu Art Museum

Kumu Art Museum is the biggest art museum in Estonia. It is located in Kadriorg Park, and it houses a collection of Estonian and international art from the 18th century to the present day.

- The museum's collection spans from the 18th century to the present day, and it includes works by Estonian artists such as Konrad Mägi, Eduard Wiiralt, and Jaan Toomik, as well as international artists such as Pablo Picasso, Vincent van Gogh, and Andy Warhol.
- Kumu Art Museum is a great place to learn about the history of art and to see some of the most iconic works of art from around the world.

Telliskivi Creative City

Telliskivi Creative City is a former industrial area that has been transformed into a creative hub. It is home to several art galleries, design studios, and shops. Telliskivi Creative City is a great place to see some of the best of Tallinn's contemporary art and design.

- The area is home to several creative businesses, including design studios, fashion brands, and technology companies.
- Telliskivi Creative City is also a great place to find unique souvenirs and gifts. Several shops in Telliskivi Creative City sell handmade goods, clothing, and accessories.

Seaplane Harbour

Seaplane Harbour is a former Soviet seaplane base that has been converted into a museum. The museum tells the story of the history of seaplanes, and it also houses several aircraft and exhibits.

Seaplane Harbour is a great place to learn about the history of aviation and to see some of the most iconic seaplanes ever built.

- The museum has several aircraft on display, including seaplanes, biplanes, and helicopters.
- Seaplane Harbour is also a great place to take a boat tour of the harbor.

Estonian Open Air Museum

Estonian Open Air Museum is an open-air museum that recreates the traditional Estonian way of life. The museum is located in Rocca al Mare, and it has several farmhouses, workshops, and other buildings. Estonian Open Air Museum is a great place to learn about Estonian history and culture.

- The museum has several farmhouses, workshops, and other buildings that have been transported to the museum from all over Estonia.

- The museum also has several costumed interpreters who can tell you about the history of the buildings and the people who lived in them.

Lahemaa National Park

Lahemaa National Park is a national park located in northern Estonia. The park is home to a variety of landscapes, including forests, beaches, and lakes. Lahemaa National Park is a great place to go hiking, camping, and fishing.

- The park has several hiking trails that lead through forests, beaches, and lakes.
- There are also several campsites in Lahemaa National Park, so you can stay overnight and enjoy the beauty of the park.

St. Catherine's Church

St. Catherine's Church is a 13th-century church located in the Old Town of Tallinn. The church is a beautiful example of Gothic architecture, and it is one of the most popular tourist destinations in Tallinn.

- The church has a tall spire and several stained glass windows.
- The church is also home to several historical artifacts, including a 15th-century altarpiece.

Raeapteek

Raeapteek is the oldest pharmacy in Tallinn, Estonia. It has been in business since 1422, making it one of the oldest continuously operating pharmacies in Europe.

The pharmacy was originally founded by a German merchant named Johann Burchart. Burchart was a member of the town council, and he was also a pharmacist. He built the pharmacy on the site of an old brewery, and he named it the "Town Hall Pharmacy."

Raeapteek has been through several changes over the centuries. It was destroyed by fire in 1625, but it was rebuilt the following year. The pharmacy was also nationalized in 1940, but it was returned to the Burchart family in 1991.

Today, Raeapteek is a popular tourist destination. It is still a working pharmacy, but it also has a museum that tells the history of the pharmacy and the art of pharmacy. The museum is open to the public, and it is a great place to learn about the history of medicine and pharmacy.

Raeapteek is a beautiful example of medieval architecture. The pharmacy has a timber-framed facade, and it is decorated with several sculptures. The interior of the pharmacy is also beautiful, and it is home to several historical artifacts.

While visiting Tallinn, I highly recommend visiting Raeapteek. It is a fascinating place to learn about the history of pharmacy and medicine.

Chapter 4:

Outdoor And Sporting Activities in Tallinn

Hiking

Tallinn is a great city for hiking, with a variety of trails to choose from, ranging from easy to challenging. Whether you're looking for a stroll through the woods or a more strenuous hike to a hilltop viewpoint, you're sure to find a trail that's perfect for you.

Here are a few of the best hiking trails in Tallinn:

- **Kadriorg Park:** This beautiful park is home to several hiking trails, ranging from easy to moderate. You can walk through the park's gardens, forests, and ponds, or you can climb to the top of Toompea Hill for stunning views of the city.

- **Rocca al Mare:** This coastal park is home to several hiking trails, including the Rocca al Mare Nature Trail and the Seashore Trail. The Rocca al Mare Nature Trail takes you through forests, meadows, and a bog, while the Seashore Trail follows the coast of the Baltic Sea.
- **Harku Forest:** This large forest is home to several hiking trails, including the Harku Nature Trail and the Harku Hiking Trail. The Harku Nature Trail takes you through a variety of forest habitats, while the Harku Hiking Trail is a more challenging trail that leads to the top of Harku Hill.
- **Pääsküla Bog:** This blog is a great place to go hiking if you're looking for a unique and challenging experience. The bog is home to a variety of plants and animals, and the trials are often wet and muddy.

- **Nõmme:** This district of Tallinn is home to several hiking trails, including the Nõmme Hiking Trail and the Nõmme Landscape Trail. The Nõmme Hiking Trail takes you through forests, meadows, and parks, while the Nõmme Landscape Trail follows the ridges of the Nõmme Hills.

If you're looking for a guided hike, several companies offer hiking tours in Tallinn. These tours are a great way to learn about the city's history and nature, and they can also be a lot of fun.

No matter what your level of experience or fitness, you're sure to find a hiking trail in Tallinn that's perfect for you.

Cycling

Cycling is a great way to explore Tallinn and get some exercise at the same time. There are several dedicated bike paths in the city, as well as some off-road trails if you're looking for a challenge.

One popular cycling route is the Kadriorg Ring Road. This 4.5-kilometer loop takes you through Kadriorg Park, which is a beautiful park with gardens, forests, and ponds. You can also cycle along the coast of the Baltic Sea, or through the city center.

If you're looking for a bike rental, several companies offer them. You can also rent a bike from the City of Tallinn's public bike-sharing system, called Ühistransport.

Stand-Up Paddleboarding

Stand-up paddleboarding is a great way to get out on the water and enjoy the views of Tallinn. You can paddle board on the Baltic Sea or one of the city's many lakes.

One popular place to stand-up paddleboard is in the Pärnu Bay. This bay is located just outside of Tallinn, and it's a great place to relax and enjoy the scenery.

Kayaking

Kayaking is another great way to get out on the water and explore Tallinn. You can kayak on the Baltic Sea, or one of the city's many rivers.

One popular place to kayak is in the Old Town. This is a great way to see the city from a different perspective, and it's also a lot of fun.

Go for a walk or run on the seawall

The seawall is a great place to go for a walk or run. It offers stunning views of the Baltic Sea, and it's a great way to get some exercise.

The seawall is located in Pärnu Bay. It's a long and winding path, so you can go for as long or as short of a walk or run as you like.

Play frisbee golf

Frisbee golf is a fun and challenging game that can be played in Tallinn. There are several frisbee golf courses in the city, including the Kadriorg Disc Golf Park and the Harku Disc Golf Park.

Watch football (soccer) match

Football (soccer) is a popular sport in Tallinn, and there are several clubs that you can watch. One popular club is FC Flora, which plays in the Estonian Premier League.

Go to a concert at Telliskivi Creative City

Telliskivi Creative City is a great place to go to a concert. There are several different venues in the complex, and they host a variety of concerts throughout the year.

Visit a museum or gallery

Tallinn is home to several museums and galleries, so you're sure to find something to interest you. Some of the most popular museums are explained above

Go on a Segway tour

A Segway tour is a great way to see the city and get some exercise at the same time. You'll be able to see all the major sights, from the Old Town to the Seaplane Harbour.

Take a boat trip to the islands

There are several islands just off the coast of Tallinn, and they're a great place to visit. You can take a boat trip to the islands and explore them at your own pace.

Go ice skating

In the winter, you can go ice skating in one of Tallinn's many parks. This is an excellent way to get some exercise while still enjoying the winter weather.

Try a traditional Estonian restaurant

Estonian cuisine is a blend of different influences, including Russian, German, and Scandinavian. You can try a variety of traditional Estonian dishes, such as mulgikapsad (sauerkraut with pork), pelmeenid (dumplings), and kartulipuder (potato porridge).

Go to a theater or opera

Tallinn has a thriving theater scene, and there are several different theaters to choose from. You can see a play, an opera, a ballet, or a concert.

These are just a few of the many indoor activities that you can enjoy in Tallinn. So get out there and explore!

Chapter 5:

Best Restaurants and Bars in Tallinn

Tallinn's culinary scene is a vibrant fusion of traditional Estonian dishes, international influences, and contemporary gastronomy. You'll find a wide array of restaurants, cafes, and street food vendors offering a range of flavors to satisfy every palate.

Let's start with traditional Estonian cuisine, which draws inspiration from the country's natural resources and historical roots. One iconic dish you must try is the hearty and comforting "Estonian black bread." Made from rye flour and fermented for a rich flavor, it is often served with butter or as a base for open-faced sandwiches, known as "võileib." Another beloved Estonian dish is "kartulipuder ja verbivores" - mashed potatoes with blood sausage.

This hearty combination is commonly enjoyed during the winter holidays and showcases the country's affinity for simple, hearty flavors.

For seafood lovers, Tallinn offers an abundance of fresh and delicious options. Look out for "kiluvõileib" - a traditional sandwich made with marinated Baltic herring, onions, and sour cream, served on rye bread. It's a true taste of the Baltic Sea!

Tallinn's dining scene also embraces international flavors, with a wide range of cuisines to explore. From Italian trattorias to Asian fusion restaurants, you'll find something to satisfy any craving. Venture into the Old Town or trendy neighborhoods like Kalamaja and Telliskivi to discover hidden gems serving up flavors from around the world.

I encourage you to delve into the street food culture of Tallinn. Head to the popular Balti Jaama Turg (Baltic Station Market) or Telliskivi Creative City, where food trucks and market stalls offer an array of delicious treats. Indulge in "karask" - a traditional Estonian flatbread, or try "kama" - a unique Estonian dessert made from roasted grains.

To complement your culinary adventure, be sure to sample some of Tallinn's local beverages. Start with "Kali," a fermented beverage made from rye bread that has a slightly sour and refreshing taste. For something stronger, try "Vana Tallinn," a traditional Estonian liqueur with a blend of rum, spices, and citrus flavors.

When it comes to dining in Tallinn, you'll find options to suit every budget and preference. From cozy family-run eateries to upscale fine dining establishments, the city offers a diverse range of dining experiences.

To truly immerse yourself in Tallinn's culinary scene, consider joining a food tour or cooking class. These experiences provide a deeper understanding of local ingredients, cooking techniques, and cultural traditions, allowing you to create lasting memories while discovering new flavors.

Whether you're seeking traditional dishes or exploring global cuisines, Tallinn's vibrant food scene has something for everyone. So, embark on a gastronomic adventure and let your taste buds discover the rich flavors and culinary traditions that make Tallinn a food lover's paradise.

Olde Hansa

Olde Hansa is a medieval-themed restaurant located in the heart of the Old Town, and it's a truly unique dining experience.

The building that Olde Hansa is housed in is a 15th-century merchant's house, so the interior is really atmospheric. The walls are exposed beams, the furniture is made of wood, and there are candles everywhere. The staff are all dressed in period costumes, and they even speak in a medieval dialect. The food at Olde Hansa is based on recipes from the 15th century, so it's all very hearty and flavorful. There's a wide variety of dishes to choose from, including roast meats, game, fish, and vegetables. Everything is cooked over an open fire, so it's all nice and smoky.

Some of the best dishes at Olde Hansa include the roast suckling pig with plum sauce, the smoked eel with horseradish, and the venison stew with lingonberries. But really, you can't go wrong with anything on the menu.

The prices at Olde Hansa are a bit on the high side, but I think it's worth it for the experience. A main course will typically cost around €25-€30, and a dessert will cost around €10.

If you're looking for a unique and authentic dining experience, then I highly recommend Olde Hansa.

It's a bit of a tourist trap, but it's definitely worth a visit if you're in Tallinn.

Here are some other things to know about Olde Hansa:

- The restaurant is open from 12 pm to 11 pm, seven days a week.
- Reservations are recommended, especially during peak season.
- There is a dress code, so you'll need to wear something smart-casual.
- There is a bar area where you can enjoy drinks before or after your meal

Bottleneck

Bottleneck is a modern European restaurant located at 6 Suur-Karja, Tallinn, in the heart of Tallinn's Old Town. The restaurant is housed in a beautiful 19th-century building that was once a wine cellar. The interior of the restaurant is stylish and modern, with exposed brick walls, hardwood floors, and a large wine cellar.

The food at Bottleneck is creative and delicious. The menu changes seasonally, but you can always expect to find fresh, local ingredients used in innovative ways. Some of the signature dishes include the roasted monkfish with black truffle risotto, the grilled lamb chops with mint pesto, and the chocolate lava cake with vanilla ice cream.

The wine list at Bottleneck is extensive, with over 1,000 wines from around the world. The staff are happy to help you choose the perfect wine to pair with your meal.

Bottleneck is a bit on the high side, but the food and wine are worth it. A main course will typically cost around €30-€40, and a bottle of wine will cost around €50-€100.

If you want a genuinely unique eating experience, I suggest Bottleneck. It's a bit of an outlay, but it's well worth it. Bottleneck is open seven days a week from 6 p.m. to 11 p.m. Reservations are strongly advised, particularly during high season. There is a dress code, so you should dress smart-casual. You can grab a drink before or after your meal in the modest bar area. Bottleneck has appeared in several international newspapers, including The New York Times, The Wall Street Journal, and Food & Wine.

F-Hoone

F-Hoone is a casual eatery located in the Telliskivi Creative City district of Tallinn. The restaurant is housed in a former industrial building, and the interior has been designed to reflect the industrial heritage of the space. The walls are exposed brick, the furniture is made of reclaimed wood, and there are large windows that let in plenty of natural light. The food at F-Hoone is modern Estonian cuisine with a focus on fresh, local ingredients. The menu changes seasonally, but you can always expect to find dishes like grilled fish, roasted meats, and vegetable-based dishes. The servings are large, and the pricing is fair.

Some of the delicacies that you can try at F-Hoone include:

- Beef tartare with horseradish and rye bread
- Grilled salmon with fennel and lemon
- Roasted cauliflower with tahini dressing

F-Hoone is a great place to go if you're looking for a casual meal with a modern twist. The food is delicious, the prices are reasonable, and the atmosphere is relaxed and inviting. The restaurant is open from 11 am to 11 pm, seven days a week. Reservations are not required, but they are recommended if you are planning to go during peak season. There is a small outdoor seating area that is perfect for a sunny day. The restaurant is located in the Telliskivi Creative City district, which is a great place to go for shopping, art, and culture.

Noa

NOA is a contemporary beachfront restaurant in the center of Tallinn. It is located in a lovely 19th-century edifice that was once a customs house. The restaurant's décor is elegant and modern, with floor-to-ceiling windows that provide beautiful views of the Baltic Sea.

NOA's cuisine is contemporary European with an emphasis on fresh, local ingredients. The menu varies periodically, but specialties like grilled seafood, roasted meats, and vegetable-based dishes are always available. The servings are large, and the pricing is fair.

Grilled octopus with fennel and lemon, for example, is a light and refreshing meal that is ideal for a hot summer day. The octopus is perfectly cooked, and the fennel and lemon offer a hint of acidity to balance out the fish.

Roasted duck breast with celeriac and blackberries is another favorite of mine. This warm and savory meal is ideal for a chilly winter night. The duck is perfectly roasted, and the celeriac and blackberries offer a touch of sweetness to balance out the richness of the flesh.

And, of course, no NOA dinner is complete without dessert. The chocolate lava cake with vanilla ice cream is a luxurious and delectable dessert that is ideal for sharing. The chocolate lava cake is served hot and gooey, with a hint of coolness to balance off the richness of the chocolate.

NOA is an excellent choice for a unique eating experience with breathtaking views. The cuisine is excellent, the pricing is fair, and the environment is classy and welcoming.

It's best to visit NOA during a warm evening when the sun sets over the Baltic Sea and the restaurant is lit up with candles. It really is amazing.

NOA is a fantastic restaurant in Tallinn that I strongly suggest. You will not be let down!

The restaurant is open seven days a week beginning at noon. to 11 p.m. Reservations are strongly advised, particularly during high season. A modest outdoor dining area is available, which is ideal for a summer evening. The restaurant sits in Tallinn's core, between the Old Town and the Seaplane Harbour.

Kompressor

Kompressor is a pancake restaurant that has been around for over 30 years. It's located in the heart of Tallinn's Old Town, just a short walk from the Town Hall Square.

The restaurant is housed in a beautiful old building that was once a workshop for steam engines. The interior of the restaurant is cozy and inviting, with exposed brick walls and wooden beams.

The food at Kompressor is all about pancakes. There are over 20 different types of pancakes on the menu, including sweet and savory options. Some of the most popular pancakes include:

- Peekoni ja suitsujuustuga pannkoogid: Pancakes with bacon and smoked cheese.
- Kanafilee ja toorjuustuga pannkoogid: Pancakes with chicken fillet and cream cheese.
- Vaarikate ja kondenspiimaga pannkoogid: Pancakes with raspberries and condensed milk.

The portions at Kompressor are generous, and the prices are very reasonable. You can get a full meal for under €15.

The service at Kompressor is friendly and efficient. The staff is always happy to make recommendations, and they're always willing to go the extra mile to make sure you have a good experience.

If you're searching for a casual supper with a vibrant ambiance, Kompressor is a terrific spot to go. The meal is amazing, and the service is outstanding. The restaurant is open from 11 a.m. to 11 p.m. seven days a week.

Peppersack

Peppersack is located in the Old Town of Tallinn. It is a popular tourist destination, known for its medieval atmosphere and traditional Estonian cuisine.

The restaurant is housed in a 14th-century building that was once used as a warehouse. The interior has been decorated to resemble a medieval tavern, with exposed brick walls, wooden beams, and candles on the tables. The waitstaff wears traditional Estonian costumes.

The menu at Peppersack features a variety of Estonian dishes, including pork knuckle, sauerkraut, and black pudding. There are also several international dishes, such as pasta, pizza, and burgers. The restaurant also has a wide selection of beer and wine.

In addition to its food, Peppersack is also known for its nightly sword-fighting show. The show takes place in the restaurant's courtyard and features two actors dressed in medieval costumes who battle each other with swords. The show is free to watch and is a popular attraction for both tourists and locals.

Peppersack is open for lunch and dinner from Tuesday to Sunday. Reservations are strongly advised, particularly during high season.

Here are some of the dishes that you can try at Peppersack:

- Pork knuckle: This is a traditional Estonian dish that is made with a pork knuckle that has been roasted until it is crispy on the outside and tender on the inside. It's topped with sauerkraut and potatoes.
- Sauerkraut: This is a pickled cabbage that is a popular side dish in Estonia. It is often served with pork knuckles, sausages, or other meat dishes.
- Black pudding: This is a blood sausage that is made with pig's blood, oats, and spices. It is often served with fried onions and potatoes.
- Pepper steak: This is a steak that has been marinated in a mixture of peppercorns, garlic, and herbs. It is then grilled to perfection and served with a side of potatoes or rice.
- Estonian pancakes: These are thin pancakes that are made with a batter of flour, eggs, and

milk. They are often served with sweet toppings, such as jam or sour cream, but can also be served with savory toppings, such as cheese or meat.

The prices at Peppersack are average for Tallinn. Main courses range from €15 to €30. Appetizers and desserts are priced between €5 and €10.

Peppersack is a fun and unique dining experience. The food is good, the atmosphere is lively, and the sword-fighting show is a great added attraction. If you are looking for a fun and authentic Estonian dining experience, Peppersack is a great option.

Manna

Manna is a restaurant located in the heart of Tallinn's Old Town, just a short walk from the Town Hall Square. The restaurant is housed in a beautifully restored 18th-century building, and the interior is tastefully decorated with antique furniture and chandeliers.

The menu at Manna features modern European cuisine with a focus on fresh, local ingredients. The chef uses his creativity and imagination to create dishes that are both visually appealing and delicious.

Some of the signature dishes include:

- Foie gras with apple and pear chutney
- Seared scallops with cauliflower puree and black truffle sauce
- Grilled lamb chops with mint chimichurri
- Chocolate lava cake with vanilla ice cream

The wine list at Manna is extensive, with a wide variety of wines from around the world to complement the food. The restaurant also has a well-curated cocktail menu, with creative concoctions that are sure to impress.

Manna is a popular spot for both locals and tourists, and reservations are recommended, especially on weekends. The prices at Manna are on the higher end, but the quality of the food and service is worth it.

Manna is a great option for a special occasion meal in Tallinn. The food is excellent, the service is top-notch, and the atmosphere is elegant.

Grill Republic

Grill Republic is an upscale steakhouse in Tallinn's Old Town. The restaurant is set in a magnificently renovated 19th-century structure, with exposed brick walls, wooden beams, and chandeliers.

Grill Republic's menu includes a range of grilled meats and seafood cooked over an open flame. The chef exclusively employs the freshest ingredients, and all of the steaks are USDA Prime. Among the trademark dishes are:

- Ribeye of Black Angus
- Tomahawk beef
- The tail of a lobster
- Platter of seafood
- Lava chocolate cake

Grill Republic's wine selection is broad, including wines from all around the globe to suit the menu. The restaurant also features a well-curated drink menu with innovative combinations that will not disappoint.

Grill Republic is a popular destination for both residents and visitors, and reservations are strongly advised, particularly on weekends. Grill Republic's rates are on the higher end, but the quality of the cuisine and service is worth it.

Grill Republic is an excellent choice for a special occasion supper in Tallinn. The cuisine is delicious, the service is impeccable, and the ambiance is sophisticated.

Bars

Pudel is in Telliskivi Creative City, which is a cool old industrial area that's been turned into a hip hangout spot. Pudel is in a former boiler room, so the interior is all exposed brick and pipes, but it's still really stylish. They have a great selection of beers on tap, as well as some local cocktails. The prices are reasonable, and the atmosphere is relaxed and friendly. It's a popular spot for both locals and tourists, but it's not too crowded, so you can always find a seat.

If you're looking for a fun and vibrant bar in Tallinn, Pudel is worth checking out.

Here are some of the beers that Pudel has on tap:
- Saku Originaal (a classic Estonian lager)
- A. Le Coq Premium (another popular Estonian lager)

- Nõmme Põlevkivi Porter (a dark porter made with Estonian peat)
- Põhjala Must (a black IPA from one of Estonia's most popular craft breweries)
- Tanker IPA (a hoppy IPA from another popular Estonian craft brewery)

Here are some of the cocktails that Pudel has on the menu:

- Pudel Mule (a Moscow Mule made with pudel's own ginger beer)
- Telliskivi Spritz (a sparkling wine spritz with Aperol and grapefruit)
- Põhjala Sour (a sour beer cocktail made with Põhjala's Must)
- Negroni (a classic Italian cocktail made with gin, Campari, and sweet vermouth)
- Margarita (a classic Mexican cocktail made with tequila, lime juice, and orange liqueur)

Telliskivi Loomelinnak:

Located in the vibrant Telliskivi Creative City, Telliskivi Loomelinnak is a popular hub for art, culture, and entertainment. This creative complex houses a variety of bars, restaurants, and shops, making it a must-visit destination for locals and tourists alike.

The atmosphere at Telliskivi Loomelinnak is lively and laid-back, reflecting the artistic spirit of the neighborhood. The bars here offer a unique blend of creativity, with eclectic interiors and a vibrant crowd. You'll find a range of bars to suit different tastes and preferences, from cozy wine bars to hip cocktail spots.

Prices at Telliskivi Loomelinnak vary depending on the establishment and the type of drink you choose. Generally, the prices are reasonable and affordable, making it an ideal place for socializing with friends or enjoying a casual night out. Craft beers, cocktails, and local spirits are popular choices among visitors.

The Guild:

Located in the heart of the Old Town, The Guild is a charming bar that combines the ambiance of a medieval tavern with a modern twist. As you step inside, you'll be greeted by rustic decor, wooden beams, and a warm, welcoming atmosphere.

The Guild is known for its extensive selection of craft beers, both local and international. There's something for every beer fan, from crisp lagers to robust IPAs. The knowledgeable staff can guide you through the menu and help you discover new and exciting flavors.

In addition to its impressive beer selection, The Guild also offers a range of delicious food options. You can indulge in traditional pub fare, such as hearty burgers, flavorful sausages, and mouth watering appetizers. The prices at The Guild are reasonable, offering good value for both drinks and food.

Beer House:

Beer House is a lively and energetic bar located near the Town Hall Square. As the name suggests, it is a haven for beer lovers, offering an extensive menu of local and international brews. The bar has a vibrant and festive atmosphere, making it a popular spot for social gatherings and celebrations.

At Beer House, you can explore a wide variety of beers, including light lagers, rich stouts, and flavorful ales. The knowledgeable staff can provide recommendations based on your preferences and guide you through the diverse selection. In addition to beers, the bar also serves a range of cocktails, spirits, and non-alcoholic beverages.

The menu at Beer House features classic pub food with a twist. From juicy burgers and crispy fries to traditional Estonian dishes, you'll find a satisfying array of options to complement your drinks. The prices at Beer House are reasonable, making it an accessible choice for both locals and tourists.

F-Hoone:

Situated in the trendy Kalamaja district, F-Hoone is a unique and stylish bar housed in a converted factory building. This industrial-chic venue has become a popular gathering spot for locals and visitors looking for a hip and laid-back atmosphere.

F-Hoone is known for its innovative cocktails and an impressive selection of spirits. From signature creations to classic favorites, the bar offers a diverse range of drink options to suit different preferences. Whether you're in the mood for a refreshing mojito or a sophisticated whiskey, F-Hoone has got you covered.

The bar also boasts a restaurant area that serves a variety of delicious dishes. The menu features a fusion of international flavors with a focus on fresh and locally sourced ingredients. From gourmet burgers and salads to mouthwatering desserts, F-Hoone offers a delightful culinary experience.

Prices at F-Hoone are slightly higher compared to some other bars in the city, but the quality and ambiance justify the cost. The trendy atmosphere, friendly staff, and unique design make it a worthwhile destination for those seeking a memorable night out.

In terms of location, F-Hoone is nestled in the heart of Kalamaja, a trendy neighborhood known for its bohemian vibe and artistic community. The area is dotted with colorful wooden houses, street art, and hip cafes, creating a distinct and vibrant atmosphere. When visiting F-Hoone, it's recommended to make a reservation, especially during peak hours, as the bar tends to get quite busy. This ensures you have a spot to relax and enjoy the lively ambiance without any hassle.

KGB Bar is a bar located in the heart of Tallinn's Old Town. The bar is housed in a former KGB building, and the interior is decorated with old KGB memorabilia, such as secret cameras, listening devices, and interrogation rooms.

The bar has a wide selection of beers on tap, as well as a good selection of bottled beers and wines. They also have a cocktail menu that features creative concoctions inspired by the KGB, such as the "Vodka Martini, shaken, not stirred" and the "KGB Spy Cake".

KGB Bar is a popular spot for both locals and tourists, and it is especially popular with people who are interested in Cold War history. The atmosphere is lively and fun, and the prices are reasonable.

Here are some of the beers that KGB Bar has on tap:

- Saku Originaal
- A. Le Coq Premium
- Nõmme Põlevkivi Porter
- Põhjala Must
- Tanker IPA

Here are some of the cocktails that KGB Bar has on the menu:

- Vodka Martini, shaken, not stirred
- KGB Spy Cake
- The Cold War
- The Berlin Wall
- The Cuban Missile Crisis

KGB Bar is open from 12 pm to 1 am, seven days a week. They have a small outdoor seating area that is perfect for enjoying a drink on a warm summer evening.

Overall, KGB Bar is a great option for a fun and unique drinking experience in Tallinn. The prices are reasonable, the selection of drinks is excellent, and the atmosphere is lively and fun. If you're looking for a bar with a difference, KGB Bar is worth checking out.

However, the KGB Bar is a popular tourist destination, and as such, it can be quite crowded and noisy. If you're looking for a more relaxed and intimate atmosphere, you may want to consider other bars in Tallinn.

Tallinn is home to a diverse and exciting bar scene, and these establishments offer unique experiences for visitors.

Remember to check the opening hours, make reservations if necessary, and be prepared to immerse yourself in the local culture as you explore these fantastic venues. Cheers to a memorable night out in Tallinn!

Chapter 6:

Best Souvenirs and Places To Buy Them in Tallinn

Vana Tallinn:

This is a traditional Estonian liqueur made with rum, vanilla, citrus, and spices. It is available in a variety of flavors, including Original, Chocolate, and Ginger. Vana Tallinn is a popular souvenir because it is both delicious and affordable.

Juniper wood products:

Juniper is a sustainable wood widely renowned in the Baltic states. You can find souvenirs made from juniper wood, such as bowls, spoons, and jewelry. Juniper wood products are unique souvenirs because they are both beautiful and practical.

Knitwear:

Estonia has a long tradition of knitting, and you can find high-quality knitwear in Tallinn at reasonable prices. Look for sweaters, hats, mittens, and scarves made from wool or alpaca. Knitted souvenirs are a great way to keep warm during the cold Estonian winters.

Viking dolls:

These dolls are made in the traditional style of the Estonian Vikings. They are often carved from wood and decorated with colorful beads. Viking dolls are a unique souvenir because they represent Estonia's rich history and culture.

Kalevala Jewelry:

Kalevala is a Finnish jewelry brand that is inspired by the Finnish national epic, the Kalevala. The jewelry is made from silver and gold and features intricate designs based on traditional Finnish motifs. Kalevala jewelry is a unique souvenir because it is both beautiful and meaningful.

Handmade ceramics:

There are many talented ceramic artists in Estonia, and you can find their work in shops and galleries all over Tallinn. Look for unique pieces, such as bowls, plates, and cups. Handmade ceramics are unique souvenirs because they are both beautiful and functional.

Books by Estonian authors: Estonia has a rich literary tradition, and you can find books by Estonian authors in most bookstores in Tallinn. Look for books in English, or ask a bookseller for recommendations. Books by Estonian authors are unique souvenirs because they offer a glimpse into Estonian culture and history.

Where to Buy Them

Katariina käik:

This narrow alleyway in the Old Town is lined with shops selling handmade souvenirs. You can find everything from jewelry and pottery to textiles and home decor. The alleyway is a great place to find unique souvenirs that you won't find in the more touristy parts of Tallinn.

Meistrite hood:

This creative complex in the Telliskivi district is home to a variety of artists and artisans. You can find unique souvenirs here, such as jewelry, pottery, and textiles. The complex is a great place to find souvenirs that are made by local artists and artisans.

Craft Market:

This market is held every Saturday in the Old Town. You can find a variety of handmade souvenirs here, as well as fresh produce, local food, and handicrafts.

The market is a great place to find souvenirs that are both unique and affordable.

Telliskivi Loomelinnak:
This creative hub in the Telliskivi district is home to a variety of shops, cafes, and restaurants. You can find unique souvenirs here, such as clothing, home decor, and artwork. The hub is a great place to find souvenirs that reflect the city's creative spirit.

Põhjala Taproom:
This brewery in the Telliskivi district also has a shop that sells handmade souvenirs, such as T-shirts, mugs, and bottle openers. The shop is a great place to find souvenirs that are both unique and practical.

Rotermanni Kaubamaja:
This department store in the Rotermann Quarter has a dedicated section for Estonian design. You can find unique souvenirs here, such as jewelry,

clothing, and home decor. The department store is a great place to find souvenirs that are both stylish and well-made.

Disainimaja:

This design shop in the Rotermann Quarter has a wide selection of Estonian-designed products. You can find unique souvenirs here, such as furniture, lighting, and accessories. The shop is a great place to find souvenirs that are both functional and beautiful.

Conclusion and Added Essential Information

Emergency Contacts

Here are the emergency contacts you need to know as a tourist in Tallinn:

- Police: 112
- Ambulance: 112
- Fire department: 112
- Tourist police: +372 612 3500
- Lost and found: +372 612 3505
- Medical assistance: +372 600 6000
- Women's helpline: +372 5333 8888
- Rape crisis center: +372 660 3247
- Drug and alcohol helpline: +372 620 6633

You can also call the following number for general information and assistance:

- Tourist information: +372 645 8890

It is a good idea to write down these numbers and keep them with you when you are traveling in

Tallinn. You can also download the 112 apps on your phone, which will give you access to all of these emergency services.

A Simple Itinerary To Help

Day 1:
- Morning: Visit the Town Hall Square, St. Olav's Church, and the Alexander Nevsky Cathedral in the Old Town.
- Afternoon: Visit the Kadriorg Palace and Gardens, a beautiful Baroque palace complex.
- Evening: Enjoy a traditional Estonian dinner at a restaurant in the Old Town.

Day 2:
- Morning: Take a walk along the seafront and visit the Seaplane Harbour, a former Soviet submarine base that has been converted into a museum.

- Afternoon: Go on a walking tour of the city to learn about its history and culture.
- Evening: Enjoy a night out in the Old Town, with live music, dancing, and plenty of bars and restaurants to choose from.

Day 3:

- Morning: Visit the Lennusadam Seaplane Harbour and learn about Estonia's maritime history.
- Afternoon: Take a day trip to the nearby town of Pärnu, a popular seaside resort with a long sandy beach.
- Evening: Enjoy a traditional Estonian sauna experience.

Day 4:

- Morning: Visit the Estonian Open Air Museum, a living museum that recreates traditional Estonian villages.
- Afternoon: Go hiking or biking in the nearby forests and hills.

- Evening: Enjoy a traditional Estonian folk concert.

Day 5:
- Morning: Visit Toompea Hill, the former seat of the Estonian Parliament.
- Afternoon: Shop for souvenirs in the Old Town or visit one of the many art galleries or museums.
- Evening: Enjoy a farewell dinner at a restaurant in the Old Town.

Conclusion

I hope this guide has provided you with a glimpse into the wonderful attractions, accommodations, dining experiences, and vibrant bar scenes that the city has to offer. Tallinn is a place where history and modernity blend seamlessly, creating a unique and captivating destination for travelers like you.

From the enchanting medieval architecture of the Old Town to the breathtaking views from Toompea

Hill, Tallinn offers a rich tapestry of experiences that will leave you in awe. Immerse yourself in the local culture, indulge in delicious Estonian cuisine, and wander through the charming streets to discover hidden gems at every turn.

Whether you're exploring the ancient city walls, sipping on a craft beer at a local brewery, or enjoying the natural beauty of Kadriorg Park, Tallinn has something to captivate every traveler. The warmth and hospitality of the locals will make you feel right at home, and the vibrant atmosphere will energize your senses.

So pack your bags, embark on an adventure, and let Tallinn enchant you with its historical charm, cultural treasures, and culinary delights. Embrace the spirit of exploration, immerse yourself in the local customs, and create unforgettable memories that will last a lifetime.

I'm confident that your visit to Tallinn will be nothing short of extraordinary. Prepare to be captivated by the rich history, architectural wonders, and welcoming atmosphere that make our city truly special. So come, wander through the cobblestone streets, discover the hidden corners, and let the magic of Tallinn unfold before your eyes.

Safe travels, and may your journey be filled with joy, discovery, and cherished moments in this enchanting city.

Printed in Great Britain
by Amazon